WASHINGTON

A PICTURE BOOK TO REMEMBER HER BY

Designed by
DAVID GIBBON

Produced by
TED SMART

CHATHAM RIVER PRESS

INTRODUCTION

At a private dinner attended by two of America's foremost statesmen, Thomas Jefferson and Alexander Hamilton, plans were made to build a federal capital. The year was 1790 and, as inter-state jealousies made it impossible to select any existing centre, a ten acre site on the Potomac River was ceded to the government, thereby creating the District of Columbia.

The task of raising the money to buy the land and to construct the buildings was given to George Washington and he made an inspired choice of planner for the new capital when he appointed a Frenchman, Major Pierre Charles L'Enfant. He was a veteran of the War of Independence and had served with Washington at Valley Forge, a site near Philadelphia where the army had endured terrible hardships during the winter of 1777-78.

L'Enfant, who was an accomplished engineer and architect, envisaged a city of wide, straight avenues with parks and squares and a Capitol building as the focal point. Many of his ideas were, however, scorned by Congress and he himself was ridiculed. It was only after his death that this talented man received the recognition that he truly deserved. His remains now lie in Arlington National Cemetery, which overlooks one of the most beautiful and impressive cities in the world.

Today, Washington D.C. has an area of 69 square miles on the Maryland side of the Potomac River and a large tract of land on the Virginia side. The population now numbers over two million, a large number of whom work for the government. One of the United States' most recognised symbols must surely be the Capitol, whose site, Jenkins Hill, was selected by L'Enfant as a "pedestal waiting for a monument". Congress now meets in its two houses and a lantern above the massive, cast-iron dome is lit when they are in session. A statue of Freedom, crowning the dome, can be seen for many miles.

The most impressive room in the Capitol is the Rotunda with its magnificent bronze doors portraying the story of Christopher Columbus. Around the walls hang enormous oil paintings depicting important scenes from American history. It is here that Presidents, statesmen and other important dignitaries lie in State. The nearby Statuary Hall was originally the legislative chamber of the House of Representatives and it is renowned for its statues and its strange reverberating acoustics.

Washington's other equally famous building is the White House – official residence of the President of the United States. Its elaborate construction of white-painted sandstone, in the Italian Renaissance style, was designed by James Hoban, who also restored it after it was burned by the British in 1814. In 1948, the White House was found to be in a poor state of repair and during the following four years it was completely renovated. Later, much of the décor was remodelled by Mrs John F. Kennedy to reflect various periods with as much authenticity as possible. The East Room is the most celebrated and is used for weddings, receptions and other ceremonial occasions. The Green, Red and Blue Rooms, which need no explanation as to colour schemes, all contain exquisite furniture and fine paintings.

South from the White House, across its sweeping lawns and over Constitution Avenue, is the world's tallest masonry structure – the Washington Monument. This distinctive landmark boasts 898 steps, from the top of which, on a clear day, breathtaking views stretching for up to 45 miles may be seen.

The city's other monuments include the Lincoln Memorial and the Jefferson Memorial. The former is in the style of a Greek Temple, with 36 columns representing the number of states in the Union at the time of Lincoln's death, and 56 steps, one for each year of his life. Inside is the statue of the great man whose life was ended so tragically by John Wilkes Booth, a Confederate fanatic, in a Washington theatre.

Resembling his home, Monticello, is the Jefferson Memorial which encloses a 19 foot bronze statue of the 3rd President, who was largely responsible for the drafting of the Declaration of Independence.

Amongst Washington's other classical buildings are the Supreme Court, with its vast Corinthian columns, the Library of Congress – one of the world's most comprehensive libraries – and the National Archives Building, which houses America's most precious documents, including the Declaration of Independence and the Constitution.

In contrast to these gleaming white buildings is the natural sandstone of the Smithsonian Institute, begun in 1846 and named after James Smithson, a British scientist who left a bequest of over half a million dollars to the United States to create "an establishment for the increase and diffusion of knowledge among men". Although he never visited America during his lifetime his remains are now interred in a crypt beneath the old tower. Smithson's money was used to build a great museum, an art gallery, a zoo park and an astrophysical observatory.

Across the Memorial Bridge from the Lincoln Memorial is Arlington National Cemetery which was first used for the burial of troops killed during the Civil War. More recently Arlington has attracted world-wide attention as the resting-place of President John F. Kennedy and his Senator brother, Robert.

Just a few miles down the Potomac River is Mount Vernon, the estate and home where George Washington lived and died, and where by his own wish he is buried, alongside his wife Martha.

Erected in memory of the first President of the United States, the Washington Monument *left* is one of the city's most impressive landmarks.

Almost all the Presidents since Jackson have been inaugurated on the steps of the magnificent Capitol building. To many Americans the Capitol is the very heart of America, for it is here that decisions are made by the Senate and the House of Representatives. Overlooking the Potomac River, the Capitol is 751 ft long, 350 ft wide and covers an area of 3½ acres. An amateur architect, William Thornton, won a competition to design the Capitol and the plan he submitted "captivated the eyes and judgement of all" according to Thomas Jefferson, the then Secretary of State. In 1793 George Washington laid the cornerstone on Jenkins' Hill and construction began on what was to become, over a period of 150 years, one of America's most outstanding buildings.

Sweeping lawns and tree-lined paths *left* create a lovely setting for the Capitol.

Looking east from the top of the Washington Monument, the Capitol can be seen at the end of the Mall *below* and at night-time it is an even more impressive sight *right*.

An aerial view *above* of the Capitol and the surrounding city.

The Capitol pictured in spring-time *above right, left and far left.* George Washington's statue and a painting of the Declaration of Independence *below* are just two of the priceless exhibits displayed in the impressive Rotunda of the Capitol.

The magnificent domed ceiling of the Rotunda is shown *right.*

Overleaf. Two more superb views of the splendid Capitol building.

The Capitol *left and above left* seen from two different but equally attractive angles.

The National Archives *above* house America's most valuable and historical documents. Seventy-two massive Corinthian columns surround this attractive building which was designed by the architect John Russell Pope.

The most highly prized of all the documents are the originals of the Declaration of Independence, the Constitution and the Bill of Rights *right*.

The National Air and Space Museum *left* is part of the Smithsonian Institution and houses a fascinating collection of historic and technically significant aircraft, spacecraft, rockets, missiles and memorabilia. Two of the most exciting exhibits are the Apollo Lunar Landing Module and the Skylab-Orbital Workshop – constant and fascinating reminders of the enormous strides man has made, and is making, in space exploration.

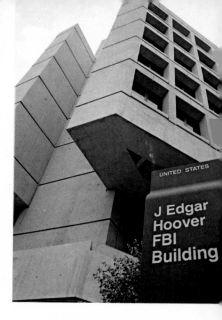

The dignified Taft Memorial and Bell Tower *left* honours Robert A. Taft of Ohio who, in 1957, was chosen by a Senate Committee as one of the five outstanding Senators in American history. Twenty-seven bells cast in a foundry in Annecy in France hang in the tower.

The modern building *above* was named after J. Edgar Hoover, a long-term director of the F.B.I.

Superb collections of Western Art, from the 13th century to the present day, hang in the National Gallery of Art. The main building is of classical design but the East Building *right, below left and below* is a contemporary structure.

Another of Washington's modern buildings is the well-equipped Children's Hospital *below right*.

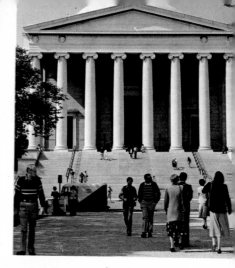

Washington's National Gallery of Art *above* houses many beautiful and world-famous paintings.

The vibrant colours of Renoir's 'Girl with a Watering Can' *left* are typical of the work done by this famous painter between 1872 and 1883.

Edouard Manet (1832-83) was one of the original members of the Impressionist movement and, like other members of that world-famous group, he and his work were subjected to a great deal of scorn and ridicule when they first exhibited their work. 'At the Races' *below left* portrays all the colour and excitement of the subject in the free style so typical of the Impressionists.

Below is one of Raphael's early masterpieces, known as the 'Small Cowper Madonna'. It was painted soon after Raphael arrived in Florence in 1504.

Paul Gauguin (c. 1848-1903) strove to convey his "beautiful thoughts" through the medium of art, by his use of bold, rich colour. His desire to obtain a simplicity, akin to folkart, led him eventually to the South Pacific where he spent a considerable amount of time, particularly in Tahiti, the Marquesas Islands and Martinique. "Self-Portrait" *above* is dated 1889.

Picasso went through several different periods, that are all clearly recognizable, during his painting life. "The Lovers" *above right* was painted in 1923 and belongs to the artist's "neo-classical" period.

The Matisse painting *right*, titled "Odalisque with Raised Arms" was also painted in 1923 and it shows clear indications of the artist's attachment to Fauvism.

Surely the most famous artist of the Surrealist school of painting is Salvador Dali, whose "Sacrament of the Last Supper" is shown *below*.

The 'Reclining Nude' *above* is by Raoul Dufy who was also a member of the Fauvist group of painters, although he did not take part in the original 1905 "cage aux fauves" – or "cage of beasts."

Mount Vernon, the home of George Washington, *left* was painted by an American artist, George Ropes, in 1806.

Another American artist, Gilbert Stuart, painted several portraits of George Washington. The particular painting *above right* was completed in 1795 and is known as the Vaughan portrait.

Thomas Gainsborough moved from his native Suffolk to London in 1754 and became famous as one of the finest portrait painters of his time, particularly noted for the grace and refinement of his work. The Honourable Mrs Graham *top right* had her portrait painted in about 1775.

Two more famous French painters are represented *right* in the painting 'Oarsman at Chatou' by Auguste Renoir and *far right* by Paul Cézanne's 'The Artist's Father.'

Another of Washington's fine buildings is the white marble Supreme Court *left and above*, which is strongly reminiscent of a Greek Temple – especially pertinent when the panels on the heavy bronze doors are examined – for they show scenes tracing the evolution of law from Ancient Greece to the present day. The Court has nine members who annually hear some 170 cases out of approximately 5,000 petitions. The Justices are appointed by the President with the advice and consent of the Senate and they are in session from October to June.

A fountain *right* outside the Supreme Court takes on a fairytale atmosphere in the moonlight.

A clear blue sky adds to the Hellenistic feeling of the Supreme Court building *left*.

The Classic style is continued *below* in the Treasury Department, which was constructed between 1836-69 and is considered to be one of the best examples of Greek Revival architecture in the whole of America.

In contrast is St John's Church *below right*, also known as the Church of Presidents – every President since James Madison having, at some time, occupied Pew 54.

The Library of Congress *right* has 35 acres of floor space and nearly 340 miles of bookshelves. The map and atlas department contains Pierre L'Enfant's original designs for Washington D.C.

Owing its origin to a bequest from a wealthy British scientist, James Smithson (who never even visited America), the Smithsonian Institution has grown over the years to include several museums, galleries, research centres and a zoological park.

The earliest building is the Smithsonian Institution itself *above*, constructed of red sandstone in the Norman style. It was completed in 1855.

In the National Museum of History and Technology are to be found exciting examples of old locomotives *below right and far right*. The African elephant *left* is in the National Museum of Natural History.

Of contemporary design is the Hirshhorn Museum and Sculpture - Garden *top right and far right, centre*. The collection deals with Western Art from the late 19th century to the present day.

Near right, centre is shown the Monument to Spencer Fullerton Baird, the second Secretary of the Smithsonian Institution.

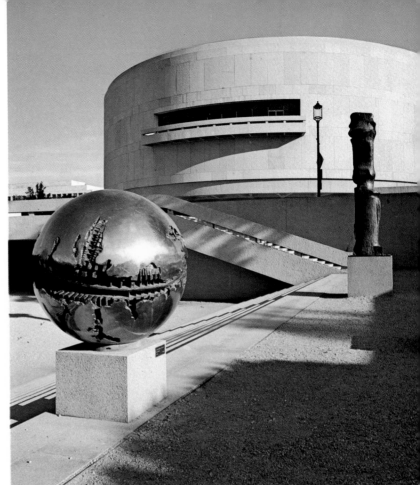

Many thousands of people visit the distinctive Washington Monument, which is shown here from different angles and at various times of the day and night. Completed in 1884, the tapered column, faced with white marble, stands just over 555 ft and was modelled after the obelisks of Ancient Egypt. From the top may be seen commanding views of the city and parts of Maryland and Virginia. Around the base of the Monument fifty "star-spangled banners" are positioned *right and overleaf* representing the States of America.

One of the most famous sights in Washington is the White House – the official residence of every American President except George Washington. The building has been restored at various times, most notably during the terms of Presidents Truman and Kennedy. The south facade is shown *above right and left.*

Commanding a fine view of the north side of the White House is the equestrian statue of General Jackson *above* in the uniform he wore at the Battle of New Orleans.

Reflected in the waters of the Potomac River is the John F. Kennedy Centre *above*, Washington's leading showpiece for the performing arts. It contains concert and opera halls as well as stage and screen theatres.

It was in Petersen House *left* that doctors examined President Lincoln after he was shot, on April 14th 1865, in Ford's Theatre. Petersen House is just across the road from the site of the assassination and it was the nearest comfortable place that could be found in which to lay the stricken Lincoln. The furniture and fittings on the first floor are all similar to those that were in the house at the time of the President's death.

Ford's Theatre, with the Presidential box draped with American flags, is shown *right*.

Washington D.C. has many fine buildings, some of which have already been featured in this book. Others in the Classical style include the U.S. Treasury *above left* and the American Red Cross Building *left*.

The enormous National Geographic globe *below left* marks the entrance to the Explorers Hall with its fascinating exhibits telling of many years of adventure and discovery around the world.

A reproduction of the famous Liberty Bell is pictured *above*.

There can be few people who are not now aware of the political scandal that takes its name from Watergate *above right*, an apartment, hotel, shop and office complex.

The National Visitor Center *below* was formerly Union Station and it has been designed with the express purpose of welcoming and assisting up to 50,000 visitors a day.

Another gateway to the city is Dulles International Airport, pictured *right*.

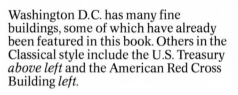

One of America's most admired Presidents was Thomas Jefferson and the Memorial that stands in his honour is a particularly beautiful one. Jefferson's own tastes in architecture, which were well-known, have been adhered to throughout the circular, colonnaded structure which stands serenely on the south bank of Washington's Tidal Basin.

The height of the bronze statue of the President is 19 ft and it rests on a pedestal of black Minnesota granite.

Engravings on the interior walls are based upon the writings of this great statesman and they include extracts from the Declaration of Independence.

From any angle the Jefferson Memorial looks impressive and it is a fitting reminder of this truly great man. From the city of Tokyo came, in 1912, some 3,000 Japanese flowering cherry trees and they were planted around the Tidal Basin. They remain, usually flowering in April, adding to the beautiful scene that has as its focal point the Memorial.

In any light the white marble edifice looks stunning and at night its beauty is enhanced when it is seen reflected in the water.

Any city, no matter how beautiful, requires more than just lovely buildings to make it come alive. It needs people, parks, flowers and shops if it is to be other than an architectural museum and Washington is fortunate in the richness and variety of life it contains.

Colourful vans *top left* advertise a variety of takeaway food and drink – just the thing to refresh the weary sightseer and, of course, there is always the welcome park bench on which to rest, take in the view of the Washington Monument, or simply watch the world go by.

Around the White House and the Capitol, the green spaces make ideal recreation grounds for a number of sports and *above* a Washington character is on hand, selling bags of freshly roasted peanuts.

Washington is renowned for its monuments, amongst them the Lincoln Memorial *pictured here, overleaf and on pages 46-47.* Designed by Henry Bacon, again in the style of a Greek Temple, the monument is sited impressively at the end of the mall, on the banks of the Potomac. Thirty-six marble columns represent the States of the Union at the time of Lincoln's death and the names of the forty-eight States, at the date of the completion of the memorial in 1922, are carved on the walls.

The statue of the 16th President *above right* shows Lincoln as a stern but just man, beset by the problems of what was a difficult period in American history.

For visitors and, indeed, residents, Washington offers a wide variety of restaurants and night clubs, many of which are situated in Pennsylvania Avenue, not far from the White House.

The city takes on a different atmosphere at night; most of the famous buildings are skilfully floodlit and the streets are brought to life by the numerous neon signs and the headlights of cars.

Part of the Washington railway system is shown *overleaf.*

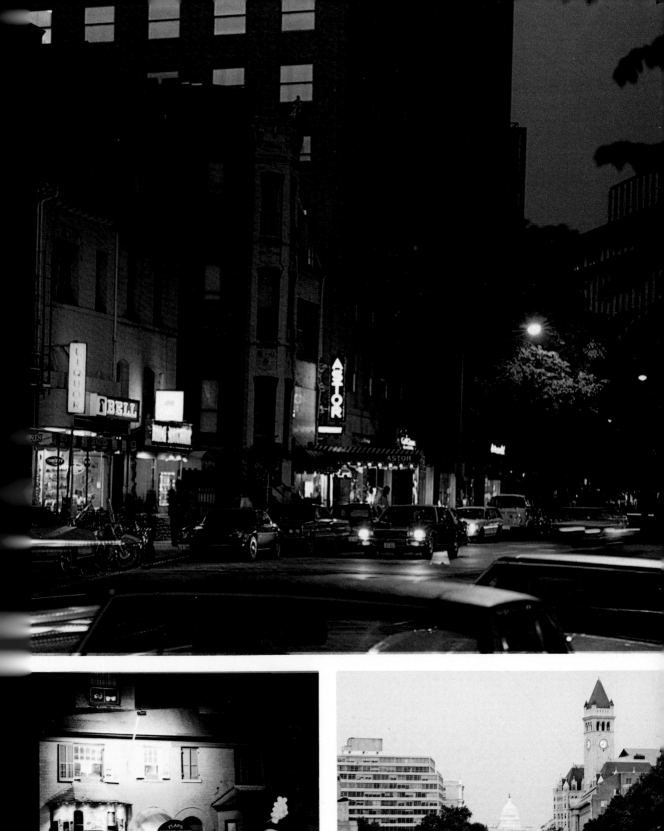

On the opposite side of the Potomac River from the Lincoln Memorial lies the Arlington National Cemetery. Within its boundaries are the remains of members of the Armed Forces, two Presidents and many other prominent Americans. The Tomb of the Unknown Soldiers – one from World War 1, another from World War II and the third from the Korean War – is just in front of the Memorial Amphitheatre.

A plaque commemorating the Unknown Soldiers is shown *below*.

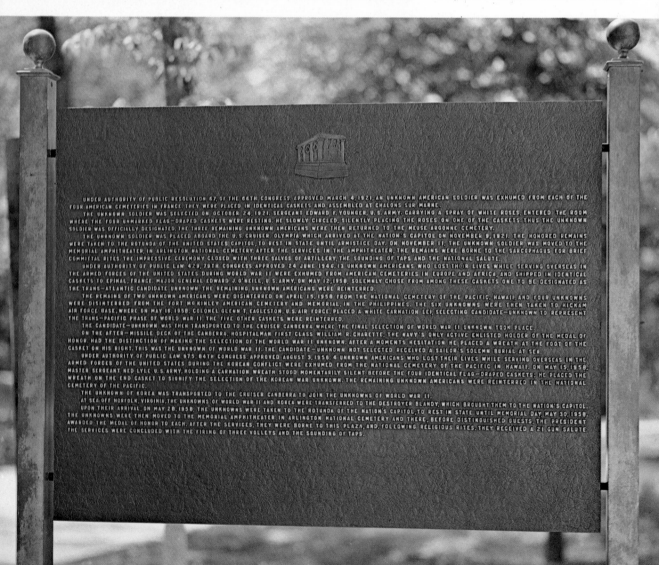

Members of the Old Guard, the oldest active infantry unit of the U.S. Army, *top left and right* stand vigil at the Tomb of the Unknown Soldiers.

The graves of Senator Robert F. Kennedy *above* and his brother, President John F. Kennedy *below* in Arlington National Cemetery.

People gather *left* to pay their respects at President Kennedy's grave.

Arlington House, The Robert E. Lee Memorial *bottom left* was once the home of the famous General and it was here that he made his momentous decision to abandon the Union and offer his services to Virginia. It is now carefully preserved and all the furnishings have been restored.

During World War II, in 1945, the U.S. Marines stormed the beaches of Iwo Jima and succeeded, after very fierce fighting, in raising the American flag on Mount Suribachi. On hand to record the historic moment was the photographer Joe Rosenthal. His magnificent photograph – thought at one time to have been posed – caught the imagination of people throughout the world. It was a picture and a mood that was very much of the moment, symbolic of the struggle, sacrifice and heroism of those days when "uncommon valor was a common virtue". Based on the subject of this photograph, the huge statue by Felix De Waldron stands, fittingly, as the United States Marine Corps War Memorial.

Mount Vernon *left* was for many years
the home of the Washington family and
George Washington is said to have
spent his happiest days here. The name
Mount Vernon was given to the estate
by Washington's half brother Lawrence,
who named it in honour of a British
Admiral, Edward Vernon, with whom
he once served.

A rare white tiger *bottom left* and
giraffes *below left* are some examples of
the many interesting animals to be seen
in the National Zoological Park, part of
the Smithsonian Institution.

All the pictures *above, below and right*
show Embassy Row, Massachusetts
Avenue, where many of the diplomatic
houses are located.

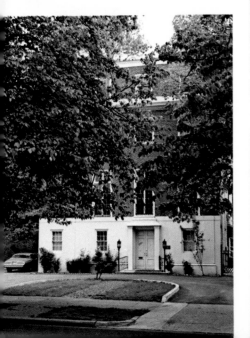

Most religious denominations are represented in and around Washington. The Mormon Tabernacle with its graceful spires *left* is situated in Kensington, Maryland. Featured *below* is the intricately designed Islam Temple.

The ornate, domed building *centre left and overleaf left* is one of Washington's newest churches – the National Shrine of the Immaculate Conception. *Overleaf right* is pictured the exquisite main altar.

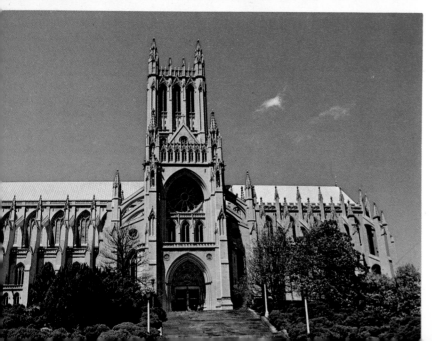

High on Mount St Alban is the Gothic-styled Washington Cathedral *left* begun nearly fifty years ago and only now nearing completion. One of the loveliest altars is in the Church of Mount Saint Sepulchre *right* – a faithful copy of the orginal in Jerusalem.

Washington Cathedral's stained glass windows *shown on page 64* are renowned throughout the world for their original and vibrant colours.

First published in Great Britain by Colour Library Books Ltd
© Illustrations and text: Colour Library Books Ltd
Printed and bound in Barcelona, Spain by Jisa-Rieusset.
This 1984 edition published by Chatham River Press,
a division of Arlington House, Inc.
Distributed by Crown Publishers, Inc., One Park Avenue,
New York, New York 10016
CHATHAM RIVER PRESS